TAROT FORECASTS 2018
PISCES

Karmel Nair was born a Catholic, is married to a Hindu and practises the Buddhist way of life. She worked in a media house and was a successful radio jockey with leading radio stations before she embarked on a career in tarot fortune-telling. It was through a chance meeting that she encountered tarot. As she delved deeper into the tarot world, Karmel discovered her intuitive powers. Tarot led her to what she describes as the most magnificent discovery of her life – Vipassana (the study and practice of mindfulness), which helped her deal with the persistent vacuum she felt in her life.

Equipped with a master's degree in psychotherapy and her skills as a tarot reader, Karmel found herself in a position to help people know what the future had in store for them, and to mitigate the negatives through corrective measures.

Tarot Forecasts 2018: Pisces is not only a book about the future, it is also a medium to change it through spiritual realization by harnessing the power of the being within us.

TAROT FORECASTS 2018
PISCES

KARMEL NAIR

First published in India in 2017 by Harper Element
An imprint of HarperCollins *Publishers*

P-ISBN: 978-93-5277-082-3
E-ISBN: 978-93-5277-083-0

2 4 6 8 10 9 7 5 3 1

HarperCollins *Publishers*
A-75, Sector 57, Noida, Uttar Pradesh 201301, India
1 London Bridge Street, London, SE1 9GF, United Kingdom
2 Bloor Street East, Toronto, Ontario M4W 1A8, Canada
Lvl 13, 201 Elizabeth Street (PO Box A565, NSW, 1235), Sydney
NSW 2000, Australia
195 Broadway, New York, NY 10007, USA

Typeset in 10/12.5 Adobe Caslon Pro
By Saanvi Graphics Noida

Printed and bound at
Thomson Press (India) Ltd

'Om mani padme hum'

'With constant practice of mindfulness you can transform the impure body, speech and mind into the pure body, speech and mind of a Buddha.'

– Anonymous

What's Inside

I

Rediscovering Myself While Discovering Tarot

They say a journey of a thousand miles begins with a single step. There I was on a pleasant Goan evening right in the middle of a bustling flea market. The stall in front of me was nondescript yet alluring, with bold letters, inviting visitors to 'KNOW YOUR DESTINY WITH TAROT'. I took the initial step with trepidation and curiosity, with the keenness to know what was in store for me. I entered the stall and met an elderly woman whose hypnotic and magical eyes belied her age. I took a seat right in front of her. She immediately asked me in a confident tone, 'What would you like to know?' Since this was my first experience of this kind, and I was a novice at asking questions about my future, I had to muster up my courage to ask: 'What do you see in my near future?' She shuffled five cards three to four times and spread them out in a circular shape. The cards looked colourful and interesting, almost magical.

The elderly woman appeared lost in the cards which made me wonder, 'Was it good or bad?' Eventually I interrupted the silence and asked, 'So what do you see?' To this she answered, 'My dear, I am happy to tell you that I see you getting married to your boyfriend, the one you are seeing now, in less than a year.' This came as a surprise to me as I was unsure of my current relationship and definitely wasn't considering marriage anytime soon. 'I see a new beginning,' she continued, 'a beautiful one, but this comes at a price.'

'What beginning and what price?' I asked. 'I see you starting a journey that you have never undertaken before, a journey that will change your life and your life's purpose, but at a price that you may have to pay now. The price is at the cost of your existing job. You may be asked to leave what you believe is your dream job, only to begin the real journey of your life.' This prediction disappointed me. I loved my job as a radio jockey with a leading radio station. I was doing exceedingly well and there was talk that I would be moved to prime time, which would be an indirect promotion. It was out of the question that I would be asked to leave and I myself had no intention of leaving. So what journey was I going to start? Losing interest, I ended my tarot reading and bid adieu to the mystical woman.

When I returned to work, everything looked normal and continued in this way for a few days. Then something strange happened. Without prior notice, I was asked to leave my current position because the project I was working on had moved to some other location and they didn't need me any longer. This shattered my dream of moving to prime time shows. That's when the tarot reader's predictions rang like a warning bell in my head. I realized that her predictions were coming true. I felt this deep in my heart. As it turned out, four months later I was engaged to my boyfriend and after another three months I got married to him.

Today, I am happily married and leading a remarkable life in which I discover something new about myself every day. Everything the tarot reader had predicted came true, but I found it difficult to accept this reality, or to even acknowledge it. After a couple of months I went back to Goa to look for her because the urge to know what she had left unsaid nagged me. She had mentioned a new journey. What could it be? Fortunately for me, I met her in Goa just as she was packing up to move permanently to Europe. I reminded her about my visit and told her that she had predicted everything correctly. 'You will discover yourself through your instinct and intuition. You are meant to do something related to foretelling the destiny of others. Your calling is to see the unknown,' she told me ambiguously. I pondered over her words on my return home from Goa.

Eventually I found a job, and became absorbed with marriage and my new life, but once in a while, I would be reminded about what the tarot reader had said about my self-discovery. Her words especially nagged me when two of my friends got engaged to each other. I had an uncomfortable feeling about their upcoming marriage and would often discuss it with my husband. I felt strongly that their marriage wouldn't last long. Since I didn't have anything concrete to go on besides my intuition, I didn't take any action. As it turned out, my friends got married and three months later were separated. This didn't come as a surprise to me for I knew something was wrong, my intuition had told me so.

After a while I predicted India's victory in a critical match, a victory which seemed impossible. Again it was my intuition, my sixth sense. It didn't stop at this. Inexplicably, I continued predicting big and small incidents of this kind. A colleague of mine was going through a difficult financial situation; I predicted an unexpected sum of money for him, a windfall. Of course he didn't believe me when I said help would come; I didn't know from where or how it would come, but I knew it would, and it did. Incidents like these would keep bringing me back to the tarot reader's prediction and that's when it dawned on me that tarot could be the missing link in my life.

I realized that with tarot I could foretell someone's destiny, heal his or her life, and show people the way forward. This is when my journey into the tarot world began.

I started learning whatever I could about tarot cards. I knew their underlying power but I realized my success lay in becoming not just an ordinary tarot reader, but a good one. I dedicated my free time to its understanding and study while half-heartedly continuing with my job. I was convinced that tarot was the big change that the reader I had met in Goa had predicted for me, and I had to master it; my destiny rested upon it.

There has been no looking back for me since I embarked on my tarot journey. Tarot has opened more doors for me than I thought possible. It has shown me the way to spirituality. Spirituality is about connecting with your real self, with the being in you. I am yet to get there but the journey has begun. Tarot has opened the door to achieving greatness and success beyond the material wonders of life. During my tarot journey, I discovered Vipassana, too. Vipassana is a scientific form of meditation which releases negative energy from your body and brings your mind, which is your most formidable opponent, under your complete control. I attended a ten-day Vipassana course which opened my third eye. It helped me understand my purpose in life – to guide others to their destiny through tarot.

Subsequently, I studied psychotherapy and counselling and this equipped me with a deep and scientific understanding of the human mind, and enabled me to understand my clients' needs beyond just pure tarot reading. Today, tarot is an intrinsic part of my life and not just a medium to predict the future. As a student and practitioner of tarot, I have learnt that there is more to an individual than just his/her future.

My experience over the years has shown me it is not just tarot readings that draw people back to me but the whole process of change that tarot offers. Tarot equips you to cope with the ups and downs of life by guiding you through predictions for the future, and by helping you harness your spiritual powers to address this future. Thus, tarot offers a trilogy of benefits – it reveals the future, it enables you to change the future and it provides a path to spirituality.

II

More About Tarot

Tarot consists of seventy-eight cards which are believed to have predictive powers. When these cards come into contact with the individual's psychic powers, they become a tool that can reveal the past and present, and predict the future. However, tarot was not always used as a tool to foretell one's destiny; it got its occult value much later. Tarot is useful in many ways but in my opinion, it has three primary benefits. Let's look at these benefits in detail.

Tarot as a Medium for Prediction

This is the first and most important aspect of tarot, and also the most attractive. Tarot can predict your entire future in a single sitting. Clients typically come to me with their problems, issues or confusions and tarot offers them a sneak peek into what awaits them with respect to their questions. This prepares them for every eventuality. To explain this better let me narrate a few real-life stories.

I had a client who visited me just once. It's difficult to forget her because of the condition she was in when she came to me to ask about her marriage. She was thirty-six years old, had a string of failed relationships and had lost faith in finding the right match for herself. Her parents were desperately seeking a bridegroom for her through various matrimonial portals. She was convinced that because of her age her chances of getting married were bleak. When she came to me she was dejected, lost and tired; the process of making her past relationships last and the ongoing process of finding a bridegroom had drained her completely. She wanted to know if she would ever get married and live happily.

My reading of her cards showed she would get married within six months. Since this sounded unbelievable to her at that time, she took the reading with a pinch of salt. A few months later, I received an email from her. She was getting married and that too, within the time I had predicted. In this instance, tarot served purely as a tool to predict the client's future.

In another case related to future predictions, a client who visited me often had just one desire – to buy an apartment of his own in Mumbai. His salary was meagre but this was his only dream and vision for the future. On reading his cards, I told him it would be another two years before he could fulfil his desire. To my dismay, he wouldn't believe me. He continued to visit me while his finances dipped or improved. Given his financial position, the purchase of an apartment seemed unrealistic for him. But believe it or not, two years later he succeeded in buying his dream apartment on his own. The prediction was as real as his home.

Tarot Gives You the Power to Change Your Reading to Achieve the Desired Results

Tarot's potential is not limited to merely predicting your future or reading the past. It goes beyond that. When a prediction is made by a tarot reader, there is a possibility that the prediction may undergo change and become the opposite of what was predicted. This primarily happens because tarot is the only form of occult or a medium which gives you the flexibility to change what you don't like about your reading. When something negative is predicted for you, you have the time to invest your efforts and energy to bring about a change in the reading and achieve the desired results.

Tarot thus gives you the power to change your life and shape it the way you want to. It will show you where you stand at the present moment and what your future looks like based on your present actions and aura. If you like the prediction, you don't have to do anything; if you don't like it, you can change your actions before the predictions are manifested. Tarot therefore, serves as a guideline to show you what you can do to improve your future by changing your present. Some of my clients feel happy when their readings go wrong, because through their effort they are able to get the outcome that they originally desired.

Three years ago, I had a client who was studying chartered accountancy and was preparing for his intermediate exams. He was confident when he came to me; his questions revolved around the jobs he would get after completing CA. However, when I did his reading he was shocked. His cards revealed that he would fail his intermediate exams; his plans would undergo a complete downturn. I explained to him that his present efforts weren't enough to help him clear the exam and that instead of dreaming about the future he needed to dedicate all his time and effort to changing the outcome. He called me after six months to tell me that my reading had gone wrong and that he had cleared his exams as he had planned. He thanked me for guiding him and letting him know his true position and potential on the day he had visited me, because that helped him address the possibility of failure before it could happen.

Tarot showed him his true position and its consequences if he had continued to do what he was doing. A change was needed and tarot forewarned him about it. Thus, tarot gives you the power to change your destiny. Tarot is the missing link which connects your actions with your desired future. It tells you what can be done to get from where you are to where you want to be.

One of my clients was an excellent worker, ambitious and goal-oriented. She often did readings with me to know about her professional growth and career success. However, once she came to me for a different reason. She was given a new role under a new boss. Just before taking over the new role, she had been looking forward to a promotion and a hefty incentive. But with the new role and the teething problems with her new boss, she was unsure of her promotion. She wanted a reading primarily to know about her expected promotion. Unfortunately, when I picked her cards, they gave no indication of a promotion. On the contrary, it appeared that she was set to lose her job because her new boss found her overbearing attitude unacceptable.

When I informed her about this reading, she was obviously shocked, but I quickly informed her that this was a prediction for the near future, it hadn't already happened. She had the time to turn things around by changing her actions and attitude, by working more patiently, approaching work with a modest attitude and cooperating with her new boss. Tarot also suggested that the less she fought with her boss the better it would be for her. She was advised to be more accommodating towards the changes her boss presented to her. She called after a few months. She had got her promotion in contrast to what I had predicted, but it was because she had done as advised. She had changed her approach to work and therefore, gained a better future. If tarot hadn't shown where she stood on that day, she wouldn't have got the promotion and, instead, would have lost her job.

Thus tarot gives you the power to change your destiny. Positive thinking and a strong belief system can go a long way in changing your life from the present state. Tarot is this source of positive energy. It shows you what you need to do to get what you desire. If your cards predict a certain future and it isn't what you want, then the solution is simple – what you are doing presently isn't working for you. Thus change your actions, increase or reduce your efforts as per your tarot reading and get what you ultimately desire.

Most of my patrons visit me at a time or stage in their life when they have either given up on hope or feel lost and defeated by life's struggles. Besides predicting their future, my tarot readings focus on what the future looks like depending on their present stance. In a situation where the readings are undesirable, I gently guide them to believe that they have the power to change their destiny. Tarot guides you and shows you where you will be if you walk a certain path. If the destination is not what you want, you can change your path and transform your life.

Astrology, numerology or any other form of occult mostly dwells on your life and tells you what is in store for you in time. Tarot goes beyond all this. It definitely tells you what is in store for you in your future and also gives you the magical power to transform your life. No one can take this power away from you and tarot's indicative philosophy only reaffirms this. The reading that you do can reflect this change from time to time depending on how you decide to shape your life on the basis of the future predicted in your last reading. Tarot is like a guide or a mentor who holds your hand and guides you to your success. Every step that you take, every change that you bring about in your life on the basis of your tarot readings will reflect a different and a better future. It all depends on how you use this power of tarot to your advantage.

Tarot as a Counsellor and a Way to Spiritual Enhancement

This third and last element of tarot is something I have acquired over these past few years of practice and experience. It is my personal contribution to enhancing tarot readings and their potential to guide lives. Tarot doesn't necessarily play a direct role of a counsellor or guide to spirituality but it does so indirectly, through me. When I started doing tarot, it was only limited to the two elements mentioned above – a medium to predict the future and to change your destiny by showing you the way forward. As I grew in my experience as a tarot card reader, I realized that most of my clients kept coming back to me to be healed and, most often, they came just to pour their heart out to me. Most of my experiences revolved around helping clients battle their life ahead through constant motivational talks and strategies to help them create a better life. This led me to study psychotherapy and counselling. I did my master's while I was practising tarot and it helped me immensely to shape my clients' lives for the better.

The scientific understanding of human psychology enabled me to come up with interesting behavioural therapies, methods of psychotherapy and various ways of counselling. Sometimes I deployed assertive therapy, sometimes aggressive therapy, and sometimes plain pep-talk therapy. My intervention as a counsellor started to bring about huge positive changes in my clients' lives. They developed a more positive and healthy lifestyle and started achieving more. This art of positive reinforcement and scientific intervention was initiated through tarot. It helped me become an expert at reading the minds and hearts of my clients. I struck the right chords of intuition and scientific intervention to heal my clients. This brought about a 360-degree shift in my outlook and perspective of live. I started seeing things differently.

This is also the time I discovered Vipassana, which is the art of self-realization, a way to nirvana, the method practised and preached by Gautama Buddha. This further enlightened me and opened the door to spirituality for me. I dedicated a lot of time to studying spirituality and ways to attain self-realization through meditation. During this time, I came upon various forms of meditation to heal my clients by helping them reduce stress-related problems, address interpersonal issues, and guide them towards self-realization, an overwhelming concept. I will dwell a little more on the details of self-realization in the Author's Note at the end of this book, to give you a brief understanding of what this concept truly means with respect to tarot, and how the three benefits that you derive from tarot are interrelated.

III

How Tarot Is Different from Astrology and Numerology

If you have ever wondered how tarot forecasts are different from astrology and numerology, let's unravel this mystery now. Whether you have a preference for astrology or numerology, in picking up this book, you are giving tarot a chance. I am sure you will not be disappointed.

Astrology is the study of planetary positions in relation to your birth date and time. Through this celestial study, an astrologer can predict your personality, strengths and weaknesses, and past and future events. In astrology, the sun's and moon's positions play an important role in the celestial chart that reveals a person's destiny. As these celestial bodies revolve and change their positions, an individual's fate changes too.

Numerology is a symbolic study of numbers and reveals one's characteristics. This study of an individual's characteristics helps in understanding his or her strengths and weaknesses which can then be applied to various aspects of life like work, love or health to get the best out of them. This study is done through the frequency of energy emitted by these numbers within the physical universe. The birth date plays an important role as most numerological predictions are based on it.

Tarot reading is therefore, not just about the cards but also about the reader's intuitive skills. Every individual possesses a sixth sense, but only a few develop it to reach a point where it can become a power, beyond the understanding of normal consciousness. This intuition, when combined with the mystical tarot cards, becomes a perfect tool to predict your destiny. Tarot is thus very different from astrology and numerology. It isn't scientific like the other two mediums, but it is definitely metaphysical.

What is metaphysics? It is the branch of science or philosophical science which studies the less explicable concepts, like the existence of God, what is cause and what is effect, what exists, why and how. It is the study of all reality, visible and invisible, natural and supernatural; for instance, the belief in the existence of spirits whether evil or benign, or of the origin of the universe which, despite all the scientific reasoning and explanation, still retains a tiny seed of mysticism. Another such example is the belief in life on other planets; we haven't discovered this but we do believe, or at least argue about, the existence of aliens and their UFOs.

One may not have seen God or experienced divine presence, but the belief in God's existence is strong. Consider the human soul; it has no form, no colour, but one believes that it exists. In my experience, intuition also belongs to such an area of study and exploration. How can one explain the sixth sense, the intuition that something will happen or may not happen, the intuition that guides me to predict your destiny which is inexplicable but which produces results that are acceptable and believable? This is the place where tarot fits in perfectly. It is inexplicable yet remarkably accurate.

Tarot predicts everything that you may want to know about your life. You just need to find the right tarot reader. Therefore, the accuracy of tarot cards entirely depends on the skill set of the reader. A reader develops this skill with great effort by deploying techniques of meditation, patience and constant study. The knowledge of these tools strengthens the reader's intuition, thereby helping her relate better with her deck of tarot cards and providing a prediction that is unmistakably precise and accurate. Astrology and numerology lack the mystical divinity which tarot has because of the reader's intuition. The cards whisper your destiny into the reader's mind and enable forecasts for your life.

Astrology uses planetary positions and numerology uses numbers to foretell your future. Tarot uses a set of colourful vibrant cards. Let me explain how these cards work. All the seventy-eight cards in the deck I use belong to one of the four universal elements: fire, water, air and earth. Fire denotes passion, water emotions, air knowledge and thought process, and earth all the worldly goods like wealth and health. Tarot comprises of major arcanas (major cards which predict characteristic traits and the distant future) and minor arcanas (small cards which predict recent developments in one's life). Like a normal card deck, tarot has four suits – wands represent fire (passion and work), cups represent water (emotions), swords represent air (the mind) and pentacles represent earth (wealth and health).

Unlike astrology and numerology, tarot forecasts are dynamic and subject to change depending upon the efforts you put in to change your future. This dynamism makes tarot magical and intriguing. Tarot is the only form of occult which gives you the power to change your destiny. My tarot readings for your future, as detailed in this book, are based on the twelve zodiac signs, the mystical tarot cards, and my own trained and unerring intuitive abilities. The categorized sections have been designed to make it simpler for you to relate with your future as predicted in this book. Limitations in performing individual readings have led me to this segregation, which is convenient as it clearly separates you from the rest in a specific zodiac sign. Tarot is intriguing and brings in a refreshing perspective. It serves more as a guideline than purely a medium to predict one's future. Besides just predicting the future, it offers solutions, warnings and guidance for what is to come. These seventy-eight colourful cards talk to me about your destiny. Now let's find out what's in store for you in 2018.

IV

Some Terms to Remember

While you read this book, you may often come across terms like querent, healer, medical practitioner, therapist, instructor, guide or mentor. These terms remain common to two aspects of life – health and spirituality. Health for obvious reasons – you will come upon a doctor, a healer or a therapist in the year ahead to deal with small or big issues related to health. The term mentor or guide may often be seen in your spiritual reading or sometimes also in your career predictions. This mentor or guide is mostly a person who shows you the way to your spiritual enlightenment. As I see a mentor or a guide in your cards, these terms will appear in your spiritual readings across the twelve volumes. The words may even appear in your career readings; this indicates a helping hand in the form of a senior, a colleague or a new entrant who may open doorways to new and better opportunities. The term querent means the person who poses questions to the reader. In this case it will be you.

A few other terms may also appear frequently in this book. These could be terms based on situations which occur repeatedly in your readings. Since there are just seventy-eight cards in the deck, repetition is bound to occur. However, I would like to inform you about the implications of these situational readings:

- Wealth creation: This implies an opportunity or a possibility to generate more wealth.
- The dilemma between two opposing elements: This implies two people, two aspects or situations that will be opposite in nature and may thus create confusion or a dilemma in choosing between the two.
- A sudden revelation or the ugly truth: There are certain cards in tarot that denote the appearance of truth which is usually hidden in the background. When this truth comes forth, it brings with it devastation and traumatic change.
- Loss of wealth followed by gains: This means that you may have faced some financial difficulty initially. But towards the end, positive cards indicate a positive change through a sudden gain. This instant change occurs due to your power to take control and act on the situations to bring about a favourable outcome.
- Wealth from gambling: This implies a sudden inflow of wealth that comes to you due to luck. This wealth may come from sources like gambling or lottery and doesn't imply any integrity quotient. This is plainly my way of informing you that money will reach you in one way or the other. These two could be the most probable manifestations of luck.

I hope you enjoy unravelling your future and use this information for your good. With this I leave you with your destiny in 2018. Happy reading!

PISCES

THE MOON

Tarot Trump

I will be honest with you. Pisces is a difficult zodiac sign to write about. That's because the way I see you is quite different from the way the world sees you. I perceive you as compassionate, gentle and loving – in fact one of the most forgiving of all the signs. However, the world perceives you as insane, selfish, overbearing and menacing. You are two people in one like your sign which represents two fish. You are a mix of good and bad, right and wrong, the pretty and the ugly. Only you have the power to choose what you want to be in any given moment.

I have known a Piscean man for many years. He is a special friend, and is simple, intelligent, intense, but also dark and alluring. He has an enigmatic charm and I have never understood him. He comes and goes like the wind. When he is around I can feel his invincible power. When he goes away, he leaves emptiness behind. This is the effect Pisceans have on people. The man I am describing is a very popular painter. But this wasn't the case a few years ago when I bumped into him at an institution where I counselled people. He was there for addiction. He told me how he had lost everything to his addiction.

My heart wept for him, but I knew that if he decided to turn himself around he would be able to do so effortlessly. As it happens, he did just that. I have seen him make a complete 360-degree shift since then. Today he has everything – riches, career, love and happiness. He chose to change himself and won his inner battle, which is why he was able to succeed. Like my friend, you are an extremist, either completely good or completely bad. There is no midway for your type. You can be whatever you choose to be. This makes you the most volatile as well as the most successful artist of all the zodiac signs.

It is difficult to describe you in a single section. You are multifaceted and can be mysterious and intriguing at the same time. It is not easy to fathom you and your sentiments. According to the zodiac, you are a fish, which implies a gentle, fuzzy character. You are not one but two fish, and this concept of duality links you to the moon in tarot, known for its dark energy and mysticism. It is the card which represents the other world. The two fish represent the two extreme sides of your nature – either too good to be true or too horrible to accept.

You are the sign of extremes like your tarot card. The moon card symbolizes darkness with a gleam of silver light that emanates from it. This light is what keeps you awake and aware of both your dark and light side in tarot. You are an artist or a total maniac, depending on how you accept this gleam of light and what path you choose to walk in the darkness. In my opinion, you are the most interesting card in the Rider Waite tarot deck. It will be a delight to take you through the various elements which link you with the moon card.

Take a close look at the moon tarot card. It has a bluish background. The central image is of the sun which seems to be overpowered by the moon, as though the moon is casting its shadow on the sun. There are two pillars on either side of the card with water flowing between them. Two creatures, a dog on the left and a fox on the right, look up at the moon and seem to bark out loud. A crayfish emerges from the lake at the bottom of the card. It's half inside the water and half out of it. The patch of land where the dog and the fox stand shows yellowish vegetation. The card is numbered eighteen.

Let's understand what the card represents in relation to you. The bluish background depicts your ever-changing moods. You are happy sometimes, sad at other times, and confused most of the time. The sun, which is overshadowed by the moon, brings out the essence of the card; it implies that your happy and stable mind is overshadowed or overpowered by your negative, dark and confused mind. Sometimes this aspect overpowers the sensible you; that's when the moon's correlation with you comes into being. This is the normal tendency in a Piscean, to slip in and out of extreme moods.

Of the two creatures depicted on the card, the dog represents the faithful, compassionate, artistic, genius, and lovable side of the conscious mind. The fox represents the dark, unhappy, fearful, confused, and mentally disturbed side. The yellowish vegetation signifies the earth, a subtle representation of the material world. The pool or the lake represents the subconscious mind; the crayfish emerging from it symbolizes the conscious awareness that gradually unfolds. The emergence of the crayfish signifies the power of intuition that you have acquired from the pool of subconscious which will help you connect with the larger spiritual purpose of your life. With time the depth of your inner being will unfold. This is where your deep spiritual side comes into play.

If you closely observe the crayfish in the card, you will notice that it seems to have two parts: one inside the water and the other outside it, like the two fish of your zodiac symbol. This represents the opposing elements of your personality – the light and the dark. After all, you are a card of extremes. The water flowing between the pillars denotes your journey into the superconsciousness. Note how the moonlight shines dimly while you are on the path of self-discovery, producing darkness and fear on this holy path. If you succeed in this journey and cross over to the other side of the pillars, you will be back into the brightness of the sun, the land of light.

This card is numbered eighteen and denotes emotions, secrets, lies, selfishness, criminal-mindedness, intuition, destruction and mental sickness. When the number eighteen is reduced to a single number, it becomes nine. Nine symbolizes completion, patience, harmony and meditation. In the ancient Egyptian and Greek cultures, nine was considered a sacred number. Therefore, you are a mix of eighteen and nine, the dark and the sacred. On the one hand, you are a crazily self-obsessed, intuitive and emotional person and on the other, you are the harmonious, loving, forgiving and spiritual guide.

I hope I have been successful in conveying the true essence of the moon card to you. When this card appears in a client's reading, I warn the person of a difficult period ahead, when emotions will prevail over analytical and pragmatic thinking. The moon refers to the illusionary land where you, Pisceans live. You build castles in the air, and inhabit an illusionary world where wonderful things happen. This is the place where the genius, artist, poet, actor, murderer, drug addict or the psychopath in you emerges.

The moon is this other world where good meets the dark. This is the stage when you have to make a choice between your dark and light sides. You may choose to live in the dark or sail through your subconscious pool to the other side. You may choose to live in the dark underworld but escape to a dreamland, with its fantasies and illusions from time to time. Alternatively, you may stay in this fantasy world and use your skills and talents in the real world. You can choose to live in the dark and become a dark person or use this dark world to your advantage and make the most of your positive qualities.

This is you, the moon, the Piscean; a thin line of sanity separates you from your alluring, seductive dark side.

You are a very forgiving person, someone who loves peace and harmony. You are a loyal lover, an understanding spouse, a caring and patient parent, an artistic worker. But on the flip side, you can be a menacing lover, overbearing and confused. As a parent, you aren't the ideal role model due to your addictive tendency, and you can be overly protective about your child. As a worker, if you fail to develop your genius or artistic qualities, you may end up being an average performer who is unable to understand corporate politics or fast-paced business.

You are the water element. This implies you are emotional and sensitive, qualities that make you a people's person. You have a deep understanding of human nature and are compassionate and kind. Your most impressive quality is your sense of forgiveness. You don't hold grudges and therefore, you are able to forgive and forget. You hold a special place in my heart, my dear moon, for your compassion and loving kindness. I only wish that the year ahead is as good as you are.

The forthcoming sections will offer a detailed reading of what lies ahead for you and what you can do about it. From now on you are not just Pisces, but also the moon.

As the moon (Pisces) *you have a lot waiting for you in 2018*. This book will take you through five different aspects of your life such as 'Love', 'Health', 'Wealth', 'Career' and 'Spirituality'. Additionally, I have included a section on 'Monthly Predictions' which will give you a head start into the year. I have also added a brand new section titled 'Love Compatibility'. I hope this book provides you with clear guidelines to what lies ahead.

Monthly Forecasts

A year has ended and another has begun. You will be excited about how the new year looks and what is in store for you. This excitement can lead you to chalk out new plans and means to achieve your desired resolution, or a larger goal. This section will delve into your future through a brief reading. The predictions will be general in nature. Specific areas of your life will be covered in detail in the forthcoming sections. So let's begin your month-by-month predictions for 2018.

January

I see you starting or getting involved in a new venture in the first month of the year. This venture or start-up appears quite promising and exciting. You have all the qualities needed, such as ability, willpower and discipline, to succeed in this initiative. However, you may have to make certain changes in your attitude or approach if you want to be successful. The start-up will come at a cost since you may have to take a back seat in this venture or make some other compromise to make it work.

I see that this compromise or sacrifice may seem difficult at this time, but its rewards will be huge. If you do manage to adopt this approach, I am certain you will be victorious. As you reach the end of the month, you will need to be more balanced and organized in your work. This will benefit you greatly. An elderly man could be part of your life this month. He is senior in age and status and may be a mentor to you.

February

You may face some serious stress and tension related to your work this February. You will feel beaten, battered and defeated. You may have done everything in your capacity to succeed but somehow the situation will work against you. You may consider giving it all up and escaping from this place. But in my opinion, it would be cowardly to abandon everything after having fought so long. Hang in there for a little while longer and you will see success.

If you are looking for a job, in all probability you will get an offer or something good will work out for you in the middle of the month. In case you do stay back to fight the odds, you will find that your work will begin to pick up. A man who is authoritative and opinionated will be part of your work scene this month. He is someone who can't be trifled with and is difficult to please. This person lacks tact and diplomacy and may create some difficulty for you. You will need to work sincerely to win him over.

March

You will face some adverse situations which may begin to deplete your hope this March. But the card that I see this month will renew your hope. You must stay on and believe in your dream, even if the situation seems impossible. You should continue to be positive and look for the silver lining in your current situation. Do not give up now and do not lose hope because the time is about to change.

A kind, gentle man will come along and ease the situation for you. He could be a family member or a close friend and will help you deal with your difficulties. In fact if you are seeking love, this man could be the lover you have been looking for. Your love life is about to turn magical and you have a lot to be hopeful about. If you have been considering proposing to your lover, now is the right time to do this. Some positive news will come through towards the end of the month. This news will be related to better prospects and wealth opportunities.

April

You will face certain challenges this month that will be difficult to deal with. I see a situation where an association or an arrangement may come to an end. This is something which has failed to work despite your best efforts. This arrangement could be related to your job, love life or something similar. Your decision to end this will be painful, but it will make perfect sense considering the odds.

Mid-month, the situation will unexpectedly take a turn for the good and I see money and prosperity coming to you. You will receive a hefty pay cheque, bonus or an incentive; or news of a marriage or childbirth will light up your life. This will give you a reason to cheer and celebrate. Towards the end of the month, you may feel bored and your love life may seem stagnant. You could be blaming others for this situation but, in my opinion, you must acknowledge your own mistakes before blaming others.

May

The month of May will be all about recovery and inner strength. This month will bring some respite after the tough challenges you have faced so far. I see you bouncing back from your deficits, especially in health, and moving towards stability and better times. This recovery has been possible because of your mental strength which has helped you overcome the odds that life has presented you. You have shown remarkable resilience and courage, thus you have been victorious.

Mid-month, you are likely to be doing fairly well in your career, and you will receive the rewards for your efforts. People in general will look up to you and will appreciate your contribution. If you are looking for a job, you will receive some good news. The end of the month will see you juggling two or more elements which will demand your time and effort. You could be handling two important aspects of work or life in general where multitasking is the only solution. Continue to juggle these elements until the situation improves.

June

You will need to embrace moderation to correct the imbalance in your life this June. Certain situations may be beyond your control and you may be feeling overwhelmed with so much happening in your life at this time. You must do everything in moderation and at the right time. You will be able to achieve a balance once you have managed to arrive at the right mix through trial and error. See what works for you and try to find a middle ground between two elements which may appear impossible to synthesize. But you have the power to temper them and arrive at a successful synergy.

Mid-month, you may need to choose one among various options. This choice may be troubling you. Research your options well and take an informed decision. Faltering now could land you in trouble. Later in the month, a big change may come along and sweep you off your feet. This change may present itself in a negative manner but if you trust it and adapt to it, it will lead to better opportunities. Something will end before there is a new beginning. You should believe in your destiny and go with the flow.

July

You will travel to different places and expand your network and contacts this July. This travel could be related to your work or it could be for pleasure. In either case, you will get the opportunity to explore diverse environments. Later in the month, you may decide to take a break to recuperate after a health issue, or simply to spend some time with yourself and clear your mind. This break will be good and will benefit you. The month will end with some exciting new developments. You will receive an unexpected sum of money which will be substantial. If you have your own business, your profits will be on an upswing. If you have a job, you may consider quitting and starting something of your own.

August

I see you forging ahead in your career and achieving the goals you had set for yourself. You will also travel extensively for official purposes. All this will make your work exciting and challenging. But do look out for the difficulties that lie ahead. You may feel defeated and disregarded by your seniors or people in general at work. In my opinion, you may be taking these minor issues personally. Don't make this a personal affair; instead approach it in a professional manner. This is not the time to put up fights or take hasty decisions. Stay calm and you will get your chance to fight back.

The month will end with a new beginning coming your way. You will embark on an adventurous and exciting journey. You have never done this before, and it may mean that you will have to take risks and face challenges. But this is a positive move and I know you are going to love every bit of it.

September

You will achieve completion this month in matters pertaining to your career or some other goals that you have been working on. You will be relieved when you finally accomplish this goal. You could ask for a raise now if you feel you are being underpaid. In all probability this wish will be granted. A man who is influential but difficult to deal with will be part of your life this month. He will play an important role and you will have to learn to deal with him. The only way to manage with him will be to work with sincerity.

You will face a lot of stress and work pressure towards the end of the month. You will be overwhelmed with your work-load. You must consider sharing it with others to ensure your productivity is not affected.

October

You will be doing very well financially this month. I see you spending a lot and saving even more. You may decide to pamper yourself with all the best things that money can buy. You could indulge yourself at a spa or spend a few days relaxing at a retreat. Some difficult issues may emerge mid-month and you will have to take decisions that will involve some risk. Think carefully before you take these decisions. You must listen to your intuition which will guide you in the right direction. If you are awaiting a decision related to your work, this may take longer than you anticipated. The outcome will come but with some delay. It's best to stay calm and be patient.

November

A man who is authoritative and commanding will be part of your work scene this month. He could be your boss or someone senior whom you can trust and work with. His guidance will be vital and you should let him mentor you. If something is bothering you, get to the bottom of it. I see you troubled about a decision that you have to take. You are seeking answers but finding it difficult to get them. You must consider spending some time alone in a quiet place – this could mean sitting or even walking on your own – to introspect. This time alone will definitely bring clarity.

The month will end with some disheartening news. You will be pained to receive this news which could be related to heartbreak in love, a commitment not fulfilled, or some situation which may not have worked out as planned. Whatever this difficult situation is, it will make you strong. You should rise up, pick up the pieces and move on.

December

The end of the year is here. I see that you will feel rejuvenated at the start of December and will be ready to take a chance in love again. The events of the past which may have left you shattered are now over, and you are ready for a new beginning. You are prepared to take life as it comes. Your work will look exceptionally good at this time and you will be at the top of your game. People will look up to you and value your contribution. I see you celebrating your success.

The month will end with some amount of tension. While your work position will be strong, the situation may change quickly and you will have a new set of challenges and will have to prove yourself once again. My advice is that you put your best foot forward and ensure that you are productive and your work is of high quality. You will be under observation now but you shouldn't let this deter you from doing your best.

This concludes the section on monthly predictions. Next are your love predictions for 2018!

Love Forecasts

Love is an integral part of who you are. You are born to love and to be loved. Pisceans are an excellent lovers – dedicated, loyal, artistic and beautiful. These qualities make you very alluring and enticing to the opposite sex. Your enigma, charm and constant duality make you a mystery that attracts attention and love. You can be a challenge to your partner, and he/she may love this aspect of your personality. Your love life will always be characterized by the good and the bad, stability and difficulties, a mix of right and wrong. Since love is such an important aspect of your life, it's very important that you discover what your love life looks like in 2018.

January

You may become possessive this month and cling more than necessary to your partner. Remember this may suffocate your partner and drive him/her away. If you believe in this relationship, you should behave with confidence. Trust that your partner loves you and give him/her space in the relationship. This is the time to test your love.

You will receive some disheartening news later in the month. You may realize this relationship was never meant to be and the person you so dearly love doesn't feel the same way about you. This revelation will shatter you but you will have to stay strong through this difficult situation. By the end of the month, you will be ready to give love a chance again and will have a renewed perspective and renewed hope. Draw upon your feminine energy to heal and face the facts of life. Don't get carried away and stay focused in love.

If you are a single Piscean seeking love, you will need to bring about a change in your attitude. You will need to let go of the image you have of the perfect lover or the ideal relationship. The longer you hold on to these notions, the further you will push your luck away.

February

You will have everything that you want in your love life – stability, love, respect, a harmonious relationship and a perfect lover. You couldn't ask for more. I see you travelling and exploring places with your beloved. By the end of the month, you will receive the rewards for all your efforts in this relationship. Your partner will value your efforts and reciprocate accordingly. This is a beautiful and magical time for your relationship. Make the most of it.

The unattached Piscean will be goal-oriented and determined to make love happen this month. But if someone is pushing you to be in a relationship, you will need to decide if this is something that you really want. The sooner you make your point of view clear, the better it will be for the other person. If you are the one who is forcing your partner into a commitment, I recommend that you refrain from doing this.

March

You will decide to take your love to the next level this month. You may consider proposing and expressing your love to your beloved in the most romantic way possible. I see you getting very creative and lovable in your approach towards your partner. You will have a reason to celebrate and I see you making merry at a birthday party, an anniversary function or some other event of this kind where you may announce the status of your relationship.

Towards the end of the month, a man who is senior to you could influence your relationship. You will need to balance your life and get more organized in the way you conduct yourself in love at this time. If you have been losing your focus in love, it's time you gave this aspect of your life the priority it deserves.

The Piscean who is seeking love will find answers in his/her past. Something or someone from the past may emerge and open an avenue to opportunities in love. For all you know your former lover may reappear in your life and your old feelings could be rekindled.

April

You will initiate a new beginning in matters of the heart. This may mean marriage, a live-in arrangement or an official declaration of love. You have all the qualities to take this relationship to new heights of maturity and stability. You are persistent, dedicated and loyal which are the attributes required to succeed in a relationship. Your beloved will support you fully in this regard.

As the month progresses, your relationship will get even stronger. A woman who is hot-headed, opinionated and interfering could play a crucial role in your love life this month. You must keep her intervention to the minimum so as to safeguard your love interest. This woman could be your mother, sister or a friend.

The unattached Piscean may be healing from old wounds due to a failed relationship. This will make it difficult for you to focus on opportunities in love. But if you have to move on, the sooner you recover from this break-up, the better it will be.

May

You will be strategizing and chalking out plans to work on your relationship this month. You are driven and committed to make this relationship last, and you are ready to do whatever it takes in this regard. All your efforts will pay off and you and your lover will share a strong bond of love. Your relationship will be based on maturity and understanding. But towards the end of the month, it would be wise for you to give your partner some space. This is not the time to cling to each other or act desperate. Let your partner take a break alone and you can take one too. You could also consider taking a break together. This break will be very useful for both of you and will help you get a fresh perspective and peace of mind.

The unattached Piscean will see some positive outcomes in love this month. You may meet someone exciting through your work. Keep your eyes and ears open for this possibility.

June

Your relationship will appear too good to be true this June which will be a magical time for you and your partner. You will have everything to feel secure and loved. As the month progresses, you will be even more emotionally inclined to your partner and he/she will reciprocate your feelings. There is romance and a strong chemistry between the two of you. You will be planning an event together which will give you a reason to cheer. This could be a birthday party, an anniversary celebration or a reunion.

If you are single, get ready to be swept off your feet by someone charming and intensely attractive. You will be head over heels in love with this person.

July

If you are stuck in a relationship in which you are feeling constrained because you don't have freedom of expression and can't be yourself, it's better to communicate your feelings to your partner. If a frank conversation doesn't work, you could consider getting out of this relationship. Communication plays a vital role in a relationship and it is important that you speak up as soon as possible before it's too late.

You could be torn between different elements which may be difficult to synergize. This will cause an imbalance and make it difficult for you to focus on your love life. The best way to correct this imbalance is through moderation and tempering. Try various permutations and combinations to see what works best for your relationship and promotes its stability. Towards the end of the month, I see you taking drastic measures to rectify the errors that you committed earlier so that you can salvage your love relationship.

If you are single and seeking love, it's about time you made love your focus, instead of work. If you don't do this, your ambition will keep you preoccupied, and you will have little energy or time for love.

August

Your love relationship will reach a stage of completion this month. You will have everything you ever desired and you will be grateful to the divine for your beautiful gift of love. You and your partner share a very strong bond of love which will evolve into something very beautiful and spiritual. You will become inseparable in body, mind and spirit. You will experience an awakening, and this feeling of intense peace and happiness will only strengthen your individual perspectives as well as what you have together. Your relationship will simply keep growing and reach greater heights of happiness and joy.

The single Piscean will see his/her dream come true in love this month. If you have been seeking a commitment, it will fall into place this month.

September

You can't be happier than you are in your present relationship. You and your partner share a strong bond of hope, love and understanding. You could hear some good news and be emotionally uplifted this September. This news may be related to marriage which is in your cards. Your partnership has obviously reached a certain stage of stability and security for marriage to be initiated. You have my blessings for this wonderful climax to your relationship.

The unattached Piscean will be getting ready to commit to his/her partner, but this person may not be ready for a serious step like this. Instead of pushing your choices on your partner, act distracted and you will succeed in getting his/her attention.

October

This month, you and your partner will enjoy a stable relationship in which there is mutual give and take. You will share your responsibilities in a harmonious way which will strengthen your bond of love. If your partner offers financial aid and if you need it, you should go ahead and accept it. This financial aid will come to you in return for your kindness and good deeds in the past.

Later in the month, you may feel defeated and disregarded because arguments and conflicts may arise between you and your partner. In my opinion, you are taking these differences of opinion too far, and you should bring a stop to this conflict before it turns into something ugly. By the end of the month, you will be working towards mending your relationship and doing everything in your capacity to resolve your problems.

If you are looking for love, you should focus on your love prospects instead of trying to create more wealth. Don't focus on something else if you want a stable love life.

November

Your workload will interfere in your relationship this month. Balancing love and work is going to take its toll on you, but it is imperative that you develop some sort of harmony between these two elements. You could start by managing your time in a better way and see to it that your lover doesn't feel ignored. A little further in the month, serious issues will rock the foundation of your love life.

Your relationship may be about to end or may have reached a stage when some sort of damage control is required to salvage it. If there is something troubling you about your relationship, or if you suspect there is something unhealthy in the background, acknowledge it and speak up right away instead of worrying about it. You should express your doubts and suspicions to your partner and resolve them before it's too late.

The unattached Piscean will be getting ready to meet someone exciting and interesting this month. This meeting is likely to occur at a marriage function or some other event of this kind. Hence it is important for you to get out and socialize at these events if you want to meet potential suitors.

December

You may have reached a point of no return with your partner and are ready to separate by mutual consent. You will be pained and hurt by this decision, but it is final. In the unlikely event that you don't separate, you will experience a major imbalance in your relationship. You and your partner will not be in harmony with each other and you won't have peace of mind.

A woman may be responsible for the problems in this relationship. This person could be a mother, sister or friend. The negative role she has played may be apparent now, and if you haven't put a stop to her intervention, you should do so immediately. Stay away from this woman's influence and take your own decisions. I see you ending the year on a very painful note. You will be distraught because of the constant conflict in your relationship. At this stage, it is important to avoid heated discussions and avoid taking hasty decisions.

The single Piscean will enjoy a positive phase at the end of the year. If you were hoping that a relationship would materialize, your wish is likely to be fulfilled with some important and incredible developments taking place in matters of the heart. I see that you will end the year in a relationship and not as a single Piscean.

This concludes your love predictions for 2018. Next let's take a look at your love compatibility. Won't it be interesting to know what your love quotient will be with the other signs in 2018?

Love Compatibility

This section is a new addition in the book. It will highlight the compatibility in love of the different zodiac signs. This is a dynamic section which will henceforth have a permanent place in my books. Love compatibility will give you a fair idea about your love equation with the other signs this year. My predictions regarding the compatibility quotient are based on the cards I see. These predictions made at the beginning of the year will give you ample time to bring about the necessary changes to establish a healthy love relationship.

Pisces and Aries

This is a strong relationship which has all the ingredients for success – love, passion and romance. There is balance and harmony as well as freedom of thought and expression, which will only strengthen the love bond in this relationship. The second half of the year will see even greater stability and happiness. This year will be fabulous for both of you. You should be grateful for what you have and continue to give your best to this relationship.

Pisces and Taurus

If there are problems in your relationship with a Taurean partner, it is better to speak up with absolute clarity. In fact what will work better for this partnership is an honest exchange of views. But be gentle and loving when you express your point of view. Lack of proper communication will eat you up and harm the relationship. I see that there is a need to introspect and evaluate the status of this relationship. It is best that you take some time off to think clearly; and I see you doing this. Do not be afraid or hesitant to take a break even if it is a short one, because this will be in the best interest of this relationship.

Pisces and Gemini

I see recovery for this relationship in the first half of the year. You and your partner will bounce back from your low period and begin to make gradual and steady progress towards stability. This low that I am referring to could be interpersonal problems or problems thrown up by other aspects of life.

In the second half of the year, however, you may have to watch where your relationship is headed. There could be a period when one partner may feel left out and abandoned by the other partner. This may be an emotional phase which will occur because of lack of time due to other preoccupations. During this phase, the neglected partner may feel vulnerable and could create emotional turmoil which will rock this relationship. Now that you know what is in store for your relationship with a Gemini this year, I would advise you to use this knowledge to shape your future in a desirable manner.

Pisces and Cancer

This relationship may go through a phase of conflict and interpersonal issues at the start of the year. To overcome your problems, you will need to understand when to be assertive and when to be gentle. Put your viewpoint forward but do so gently. You need to know that your partner loves you even though he/she can be difficult at times. The second half of the year will be a good phase for your relationship with a

Cancerian. Your partner will reciprocate your feelings of love and will be willing to work on the relationship. If you are burdened with work, it's time you set your priorities and made time for romance!

Pisces and Leo

Your relationship with a Leo will be troubled this year. Do not be in a hurry to take decisions or jump to conclusions. You will experience some stress and tension in your love life in the first half of the year. Be patient and avoid any interactions that may get heated; the situation will settle down eventually. The second half of the year will be a far better period for you when you and your Leoniru partner may decide to move in together, or announce marriage, or an engagement. This is a great beginning considering the upheaval you faced in the initial part of the year. Hope you stay blessed and happy.

Pisces and Virgo

If you are feeling constrained or dissatisfied in your relationship with a Virgo, then speak up. There's no point feeling stuck in a relationship which doesn't give you happiness, nor does it give you the freedom to be yourself. In this situation it is best to break free and follow your heart. Be sure about your intentions and remember to work on any issues. Remember every relationship requires the cooperation of both parties involved. Make sure both of you are committed to this love affair.

Pisces and Libra

This year will start off very well for you and your Libran partner. I see the first half of the year being a magical time for your love. Both of you will be doing well and enjoying the compatibility that exists in your relationship. However, problems will arise in the second half of the year when either you or your partner may become overly possessive. This will create an impediment in the progress of the relationship. It's best to let go at a time like this and test the strength of your love bond. Holding on to someone against his/her wishes will only harm the relationship. Win your partner's love instead of forcibly demanding it.

Pisces and Scorpio

This is a beautiful relationship and I see that you and your partner have a very strong bond of love. There will be mutual give and take which will lead to perfect balance and harmony. If your partner wishes to help you financially, accept it. This is in your best interest, and there is nothing wrong in taking help from your beloved. At some point during the year, you and your partner may be ready to take your relationship to the next level of commitment. This could be a marriage or a live-in arrangement. This is wonderful and my blessings will always be with you.

Pisces and Sagittarius

Your relationship with a Sagittarius is not balanced at all. One of you will not be fulfilling one's share of the duties and responsibilities in this relationship. A strong relationship is not simply about love and romance. You have to take responsibility for each other and this seems to be faltering in this relationship.

This year doesn't look all that good for both of you; in fact your love affair may just come to an end with both of you deciding to part ways considering your relationship has not worked out despite your best efforts. Instead of being in a relationship which has no love and meaning, it would be advisable to end it gracefully. This decision may not be easy but it is in both of your best interests.

Pisces and Capricorn

You may be feeling stuck in a relationship with a Capricorn because you don't see any scope for improvement or any future for you and your partner. But this relationship may have become too comfortable and you may not want to take the risk of leaving it. You may be confused regarding the fate of this relationship and your own future. You should take a stand – either happily stay in the relationship or get out now. This has to be your decision.

Complaining and whining will not solve your problem. Instead, take control of your life and take action that will benefit you and your partner. You may have to plan and strategize to make this relationship work.

Pisces and Aquarius

Your work is going to be challenging and will take up a lot of your energy and time leaving your lover feeling distressed and lonely. This is not such a good space to be in as it denotes imbalance, and this imbalance could lead to bigger issues in the future. Hence, focus on fixing this problem while you still have time. You may be working on something new, but don't neglect other aspects of your life like love. The second half of the year will be more positive and your love life will improve, and may even be unusually good. You and your partner will share a strong bond and will be prepared to take up any challenge that life presents you.

Pisces and Pisces

Two water signs make for a good match. You and your Piscean partner will be totally in love this year. In fact both of you may decide to take your relationship to the next level and may consider marriage, an engagement or some other arrangement to formalize your relationship. There will be happiness, love and celebration in your relationship in the first half of the year. This will continue in the second half, when I see mutual give and take. This is the best way to strike a balance in a relationship. You will be willing to give love, respect and space to each other and also offer help which could be financial aid if required. This is a great way to achieve harmony and balance in a relationship.

This concludes your compatibility quotient with the other zodiac signs. Let's move on to another important aspect of your life – your health in 2018.

Health Forecasts

Health is wealth and this is especially true for you. You have a very emotional and sensitive heart which tends to get affected more than your body. To safeguard this weak and innocent heart you have to be strong, or at least appear strong. This strength comes from a sound mind, thus you need to take good care of your mental health as well as your physical health. Let's see what 2018 has in store for your health and overall well-being.

January

You will start the year feeling some amount of stress related to a dilemma you are in. You have to choose from various options and understand which choice suits your current situation. This decision could be related to a treatment option, health practitioners or something else related to your health. The sooner you evaluate your options and make a choice the better it will be for you.

After dealing with this stressful phase, you may decide to take a break to simply relax and recuperate, or you may be hospitalized for a health condition. If it is hospitalization, it may be for a routine check-up or something minor that you can easily deal with. You will end the month with feelings of rejection, sadness and disappointment. You will be hurt with the way a certain situation has turned out. You may be taking this situation personally when you shouldn't be doing so. In my opinion, you should move on instead of getting stuck in the past and being your own greatest adversary.

February

You will face stiff competition this month which may take its toll on your health. If you are facing some serious ailments, get ready for some tough times ahead. You will have to fight the condition you are facing, and I see you getting ready emotionally to take on what lies ahead. There could be some positive news or development which will motivate you to focus on your health in a positive manner. Watch the way you conduct your body and mind and strike a balance with respect to your work and health.

The situation may get difficult as you move closer to the end of the month. I see you struggling to deal with some news you may have received or something that is likely to occur. But know this – success is definite if you stay focused and positive. You can heal and combat anything that comes your way. This self-belief is most important at this juncture.

March

You will see some happy times related to your health this month. An obstacle you faced will be removed and I see you moving forward in health matters. You will be emotionally stable and content and have a general sense of well-being. Mid-month, I see you receiving rewards for your efforts. You will achieve your fitness goal, recover from your ailments and be successful with other health goals that you may have been working on. You truly deserve a pat on your back for your brilliant effort, and I hope you continue to make progress in your health.

Towards the end of the month, you will need to watch where you are headed in terms of your thoughts and actions.

If you have been expecting a test result or a report and have been anticipating a negative outcome, change your thoughts and think positively. Stay calm and know that all will be well eventually.

April

You may be getting very restless waiting for some news or test results related to your health. You may be getting overly anxious about this outcome. But worrying and negative thinking are not going to help. It would be better to await the outcomes calmly. If you get desperate you will push your luck away. Everything in the universe happens at its own time.

There is some regret or feelings of anger and hurt which are holding you back in the past. You may have taken some wrong decisions in the past and you are now brooding over this instead of living in the present. My advice to you would be to let go of this past baggage and focus on your life in the present. Pay attention to all the positives that you have now. Towards the end of the month, your health and vitality will be at their peak. You could be working rigorously on achieving your fitness goals. But ensure that while doing so you don't injure yourself, or overdo any routine if you have already sustained injuries. Go easy on your body and know its limits.

May

You will be doing exceptionally well in May which will be marked by taking action for your health. You will be goal-oriented and feeling energetic, and you will move forward on your health goals. You may also undertake extensive air travel. But whatever you do, ensure you adopt a conservative attitude towards your health and respect your body's limits. Your health is likely to improve further as the month progresses. If you have been suffering from a serious health ailment, you should get some respite this month.

However, do look out for a predicament that may bother you towards the end of the month. You may be confused about treatment options and a doctor's diagnosis at this time. If you have any doubts about these matters, do some investigation and research before you take a decision. This stage of research and introspection will be quite difficult but you will receive the answers you are seeking. Even a ten-minute walk alone to introspect will produce some clarity and help you take a decision.

June

You will be feeling restricted and constrained and unable to do what you want to do. This is not a good phase to be in and you should try to break free from it. The best way to do this is to think positively. Be calm and don't allow yourself to dwell on your fear-based thoughts or anticipate bad luck. Mid-month, you will begin to recover from the deficits in your health.

Your recovery will be rapid and you will be in for some positive news related to a test report you have been expecting. You will be feeling rather fit and upbeat at this juncture, and taking good care of your health by eating right, sleeping well and exercising regularly. The key to good health lies in these daily activities. You will need to keep up your effort in the forthcoming months to stay fit and healthy and have an overall sense of well-being.

July

You will be on a break this month. You may take this break to relax and unwind and get some clarity in your thinking, or the break could be for hospitalization. This hospitalization could be for a routine health check-up or something minor. Whatever the reason, this break will serve you well and give you some time to relax. During this break you will need to observe your thoughts. Your health conditions are a manifestation of your negative thoughts which typically emerge because of stress and tension. Taking life too seriously and feeling defeated and disregarded by others will only make your health worse. Separate yourself from your ego by observing your thoughts and half your worries will be over.

You will feel more in control of your health towards the end of the month. I see you strategizing and chalking out plans to move ahead and set goals in health. A woman may come along and help you in health matters. She could be a healer or an instructor of some kind.

August

You need to be careful about whom you trust in health matters. Someone may not be entirely honest with you about your health condition. Another person may try to cheat you in the name of health. If you suspect foul play, get to the bottom of it. In the case of medical treatment, get a second opinion on the intervention suggested. Stay vigilant.

The good news is that despite the odds, your health will recover. You will heal from your old wounds and your chronic ailments will see some improvement. You will achieve this stability and success because of your mental strength. I hope you continue to stay strong. The month will end beautifully with a wish or something you have desired being granted. You will manifest your greatest dream in health. This will leave you feeling happy and motivated for the new beginning that lies ahead.

September

You will need to change your attitude and your approach to health to keep up with the times. If you don't do this, your health may suffer. You may come upon a change which is difficult to deal with this month, and your only option will be to alter your lifestyle and your approach towards your body and mind. The sooner you accept this change and adapt to it, the better it will be.

The good news is that this sacrifice will bring its own reward. You will receive this reward within a few days from the time you initiate this change. Your body and mind will start responding to your new approach and you will feel upbeat and healthier. Stay focused and positive and the situation will improve even further. Whatever the odds, you should believe that you can beat them. Hope and self-belief is what will keep you going.

October

Sometimes it is good to just sit back and relax instead of pushing yourself too hard for a certain outcome. You should let your hair down and have some fun, and make time to enjoy your life this month. If you are confused about some issue, follow your intuition. It will guide you in the right direction when it comes to your health. If you listen to your intuition, which talks to you through your inner voice, you will arrive at a proper decision. This may not be the time to take any risky decisions or have a medical intervention which you are not convinced about. Remove all doubts before you commit to any intervention.

You will have some happy times later in the month when you are relaxed and at peace. You may decide to go on a holiday or a vacation to rejuvenate. This will be an excellent decision considering the emotional upheaval you faced recently. Your health will be good towards the end of the month.

November

You will be motivated to take action to improve your health this month. You will be busy with tasks that will build on what you achieved in October. You have fought against the odds and made a brilliant comeback in health. This is due to your efforts and determined attitude which I am thoroughly impressed with.

If you have any questions related to your health, know that the answers lie in your past. Take a walk down memory lane and deal with the repressed emotions from your childhood. Processing these emotions will help you heal your old wounds. Dig deeper and you may find the answers to many of your emotional issues. Towards the end of the month, you may conclude an association that has failed to work out for you. This could involve a healer, doctor or an instructor. This could also imply a sudden end to a relationship based on love, work or wealth. You could be feeling distraught and hopeless because of this decision, but this end will eventually give you some respite and present you with a solution to your problem. Trust me this end will be the start of something bigger and better for you.

December

Your health will bounce back this month and you will once again be feeling at your best. You will be goal-oriented and focused on achieving new tasks and goals related to your health. A woman, who may be part of your health scene this month, will help you achieve your desired outcomes. As you move closer to the end of the month, you will be ready to adopt a new approach to your health. I see you establishing a health routine which includes eating a balanced diet, getting enough sleep and exercising daily.

Along with this daily routine, you should also adopt a more serious approach towards developing your emotional health and achieving an overall sense of well-being. This is an excellent way to end the year. However, I see that you may unleash your indulgent side in the last few days of December when you will be in a party mood. But losing focus and discipline will only undo all the good you have achieved in your health. You must try to stay focused on your health goals at this time. If you don't, be ready to face the consequences. Stay vigilant and don't give in to the weaker side of your personality. Remember health is wealth.

This concludes your health predictions for 2018. The going has been good so far and I hope this continues in the forthcoming year. Next let's take a look at your wealth predictions.

Wealth Forecasts

Pisces, or the moon in tarot, rarely has large financial goals. You are generally content with what you have and are not fixated on wealth creation. You want money in order to lead a good life but it is not an obsession with you. You don't want to acquire wealth for the love of it or as a status symbol, but for the comforts and the quality of life it can provide you. You are very clear about what you want and how much you want. This approach, which is due to your inner consciousness, separates you from the other zodiac signs. You have a spiritual inclination which influences your attitude towards material possessions. Now let's find out what your wealth predictions are for 2018.

January

The year will not start well for you. You may be deceived or cheated by someone you trusted with your money or wealth planning. There is also a possibility that a minor theft may take place in the early part of the month. Don't trust people so easily and keep in mind that someone somewhere is not being honest with you. You will have to do thorough investigation before you decide to make an investment based on another person's judgement and guidance.

You will initiate something new in terms of an investment plan or a start-up venture with an intention to make money. This is unexplored territory for you, hence it will come with some risks and challenges. But what's exciting about this plan is that beyond its risks and challenges lie big rewards. If your leap of faith in these untested waters turns out to be a success, you will receive huge returns. The month will end with you channelizing your thoughts into action. You will be ready to take on what lies ahead and make a difference in your life and the lives of your loved ones. You will be eager and enthusiastic to go forth and face the challenges ahead.

February

Your finances will be on an upswing and you will see your money grow gradually and steadily this month. Your returns on investment will be good and the other aspects of your wealth will also be performing well. There will be a perfect balance in the way you conduct your finances, and you will know exactly where your money is going and where you need to use it. This will produce a perfect synergy between your income and expenses.

Mid-month, a woman may help you out with your financial planning. She will offer you some information which may change the face of your finances. You should also leverage your creative skills at this time. Your creativity could lead to some interesting ideas that could open the door to greater opportunities for wealth generation.

March

Your financial situation is likely to look very good this month. Contracts and legal agreements which promise better prospects will be headed your way. You will have enough money as long as you balance your income and expenditure. I see that you may lose track of your spending which will cause a slight imbalance. Don't spend unnecessarily and misuse the money you have earned through hard work as this is the time to build a sound financial base for yourself.

You will be able to correct the imbalance which will cause your financial situation to improve towards the end of the month. Money will come through one way or the other. This will be a great time to earn money through investments. If you have the appetite for taking risks, in my opinion you should take the leap into the stock market now. You will definitely earn huge returns as the timing is perfect to achieve the impossible.

April

You will take up a new financial avenue this month. This will be in the form of a joint venture or a collaboration of some kind, or you may join hands with another person or institution for financial gains. This project will be short-lived but the returns will be good. However, do look out for the middle of the month when your finances may take a beating. Your tight financial situation will cause you stress and you will be worried about meeting your financial obligations. But worrying is not going to help you solve your problems. Instead, you should focus, think calmly and be positive. This way you will make some headway in your finances.

Your situation will improve towards the end of the month and you will have enough to take care of your expenses and those of your family members. You should consider saving some part of your earnings for future contingencies. The best way to attract money to yourself is to give out as much as you can with the intention to give, and not to gain from this.

May

This will be a very good month for your finances and you will strike the right balance between your income and expenses. You will be self-sufficient and you will see positive developments this month. You may consider big-ticket purchases like a home or announce marriage or an engagement which will lead to expenses that you will conveniently manage.

I see you getting lucky and receiving a windfall at the end of the month. This unexpected sum of money will come through sheer luck, family inheritance, gambling or some other source. You will have more than you need and you should consider sharing your abundance with the less fortunate. I see you feeling happy with your good fortune and in a mood to celebrate.

June

You will meet a financial adviser who will provide you with some financial insights that will help you plan better. If you haven't considered this sort of intervention or guidance before, you should do it this June. If you apply this knowledgeable and experienced person's advice, you are likely to receive financial benefits.

Mid-month, I see you focusing on the negative aspects of your financial situation. You may be thinking too much about the things you don't have and can't afford instead of focusing your energy on what you already have. This kind of negative thinking will lead to negative experiences. If you have a certain financial goal in your mind, chalk out a viable plan and work on achieving it. Don't simply sit back and procrastinate over it. In the last few days of the month, you will be eagerly awaiting the returns on your investments or money from some other source. Well, the delay is likely to be longer than you anticipated but you can be assured that the returns will eventually come. So avoid getting desperate which will only push your luck away.

July

You may feel constrained and unable to do the things you want to do financially. You may begin to detest your financial situation. Instead of adopting this negative approach, stay positive and look at what you have and what you are capable of earning in the future. Don't let negative thoughts hamper your progress. The best way to deal with financial inadequacy is moderation. Moderate your expenses to match your income. You should try to reduce your cash outflow and maximize your inflow.

Towards the end of the month, you will need to face the reality of your financial situation. The news will not be good and you will have to face the music. The best way to reverse this financial downturn will be to freely give what you have. This giving will attract much more to you. This is how the law of attraction works. Trust me and try it!

August

There will be an unexpected change in your financial situation this month which will sweep you off your feet. This change may cause an upheaval in your financial planning. It will end an ongoing association or plan which seemed worthwhile and consistent, and begin a new one. This sudden development will cause you to feel regret and you will find yourself comparing your present with the good times in the past and pondering over the unexpected twists in life which have led to your current situation.

The more you think about the past, the more you will push the good away. Accept the reality of your situation and move on. You should look at ways to salvage the present situation rather than brood over what has gone by. The month will end with some positive news which you have been waiting for. This breakthrough, which took a long time coming, will be a reality this August. I see you on an upward path and proceeding towards financial stability.

September

You should seek financial guidance from an expert or a professional this month. One such individual or institution will offer you reliable financial advice which will ease your mind. You should chalk out a plan based on this financial advice. Your money situation will get better and you will be on your way to financial stability. You will have enough money to cover your expenses and more will come from unexpected sources. This may be through family inheritance, a lottery or gambling. In my opinion, you should ensure that you plan how to spend this money considering the odds you faced when you didn't plan.

Mid-month, you will lose focus and begin to develop negative thinking. You will be brooding over what you don't have instead of focusing on what you do have. This will make you weak and you will attract negative events to yourself. It is better to change this thought process before your fears become a self-fulfilling prophecy. The best way to change your negative mindset is to adopt an attitude of gratitude for everything you possess now.

October

I see you eagerly awaiting some reward or a return on investments. But this windfall is going to take longer than you anticipated. The money will come when the time is right; desperation will push it further away. Hence, relax and know that the money will come in due course. Your financial situation will improve gradually and the positive developments which will take place this month will help you recover from your deficits.

The answers to your financial problems lie in your past. I see something emerging from your past, an old memory, an old contact or a past association which will lead to some interesting opportunities. This blast from the past holds the key to your financial treasure. You must use it and cash in on the opportunities which could transform your life.

November

If you think your financial difficulties are here to stay, and persist with such negative thoughts, what you fear may become a reality. Instead, you should try to think positive to achieve a good outcome. After all you create your reality with your thoughts. The good news is that despite your negative thinking, you will achieve a balance between your income and your expenses.

The temptation to overspend will be quite strong towards the end of the month. You may be tempted to go all out and buy everything you desire. But this could disturb your financial equilibrium. Hence go slow and be controlled in your spending. If you must spend, consider investing in home improvements. These need not be expensive and can be carried out with a modest budget.

December

I see you achieving your financial goals as the year draws to a close. The financial block you have been facing will dissolve and money will begin to come in gradually once again. But don't get carried away by your earnings and avoid lavish spending. You should use this influx prudently. In mid-December, you may begin to worry about managing your expenditure. This is the time to take action to release funds which seem stuck. For instance, if you are in a business, increase your collections and if your finances depend on someone else's decision, gently put pressure on this person so that you get what you want. This is the time to act fast.

I see some positive developments at the end of the month, when you will get the financial assistance you have been waiting for. This will open the doorway to financial betterment and opportunities that could transform your situation. You must make the most of these opportunities. But use them prudently. The year will end well for you and I hope your financial situation continues to improve in the new year.

This concludes your wealth predictions. Your career predictions for 2018 come next.

Career Forecasts

Professions that involve art, culture and writing, in which creativity and emotions play an important role, are best suited to a Pisces. You are led by your heart and this reflects in your work. However, not all of you can be painters, dancers or artists. Most of the moons I have known have been stuck in the corporate world where success depends on the approval and appreciation of others. Now let's take a look at how you will fare in your career in 2018.

January

You will need to be more organized and balanced in your approach to your work this month. If you have the tendency to be disorganized, you will need to get serious and behave in a way which is acceptable in the system that you are in. A man, someone senior and in a position of authority, will mentor you through this phase. He will take a liking for your work and will want to support you in the best possible way. If you are a woman Piscean, be wary of getting romantically involved with this man.

You are going to face some tough times as the month progresses. Your work will become challenging and the people around you will be difficult to deal with. But you will have to hang in there and face what comes your way. I see you inclined to give up and flee the situation. But this will be a cowardly move especially after you have come so far.

In my opinion, you should hang on and prove you are up to the challenge.

You will receive the rewards for your efforts at the end of the month. You will receive money and recognition for the effort you have put in. This may come in the form of a salary increment, a bonus or a promotion. If you are involved in a business, your profits may be on an upswing. If you have been considering having your own business, this may be the time to establish it.

February

This will be a good month for your career. You will hear some positive news that will lift your spirits and boost your morale. But don't take your work so seriously that you forget to have fun. Enjoy your work and learn to look at the lighter side of life. You are allowed to let your hair down and enjoy yourself once in a while.

The middle of February will be a golden period for you. I see you exceptionally happy with the way your career has turned out. In fact this phase is so positive that any wish you make for your career may just come true. So without wasting any time, close your eyes and make a wish, and wait for it to be manifested. This is the power of your wish and your positive thinking. I see good news coming your way but it will come with some delay. If you were expecting this news at the end of the month, in all likelihood you will be disappointed. You may have to wait a little longer for this news to reach you.

March

You will take up a new job, an assignment, a project or a client this month. This is a new beginning and of course, it will come with its challenges and risks. While it may appear to be adventurous and promising, it will have some teething problems.

But knowing your skills and abilities, I am confident that you will be able to prove yourself. You will embark on this journey and deal with what comes your way with a positive attitude.

You will be excited to prove yourself and will be ready to do whatever is required in this regard. You must channelize this energy to achieve your larger goals. Mid-month, you may face small issues such as a co-worker scheming against you. This person will do everything in his/her capacity to create a hindrance for you, but eventually your work will prevail. You need to focus on your job and brush away these petty issues. Don't let them affect your spirit.

Sometimes it's good to take a walk down memory lane. When you do this, you may come upon something or someone who will strike the right chord and a life-changing career opportunity will be presented to you. Something like this is about to take place at the end of this month. So open up your treasure chest of old memories and see what jumps out at you.

April

A woman will come along and play an important role in your career, pointing you in the right direction for success. This is an important time to stay focused and convert your thoughts into action. This will be an excellent development, but avoid broadcasting your ideas which will only attract unnecessary attention.

Mid-month, you will be eagerly awaiting an opportunity or a good break which you are certain will come through. I see you enthusiastically awaiting this positive development and ready to take up the challenges that lie ahead. You will be motivated, enthusiastic and full of life at this juncture. The month will end with some positive news. You will get what you want which will leave you overjoyed. You will be emotionally ready to take on what life presents next.

May

You will receive accolades for achieving your targets and deliverables this month. You will be assisted by a woman whom you can trust. People will be impressed by your achievements and begin to take notice of your work. There will be a general buzz around you. If you feel underpaid for the amount of work you have been doing, then you should speak up and ask for a raise. This is a good time to blow your own trumpet. Let people know what you are truly capable of.

A man, who may appear to be a bully but is actually just doing his job, will create difficulties for you towards the end of the month. You may be taking what he says and does personally. Hence, it is important to lighten up and ignore the unnecessary issues. For all you know, you may begin to work better under this taskmaster's supervision.

June

You will be doing exceptionally well in your career and your work will be noticed by everyone. You will be enthusiastic because of some developments you are expecting in the near future. This could be a job change, a job offer or some other positive news in your existing set-up. This will motivate you to move forward and perform better than you would have otherwise.

You should consider using your creative skills to make a difference to your career this month. Exploit your creative skills and produce something beautiful and remarkable. A woman may help you in executing this impossible feat. Remember to adopt an approach of love and respect towards your existing job. If you respect and appreciate what you do, your work will respect you back.

July

You will start something remarkable this month, such as a new venture, a job or an assignment which is exciting but also has some risks. But this leap of faith is going to pay off. You will embark on a journey which is different, unexplored and something beyond the mundane. I see you doing exceptionally well and achieving impossible feats. Victory will be yours.

During this time, stay aloof from office politics and don't pay too much attention to people who try to create an impediment to your progress. Your work will eventually speak for you. There will be a delay in some opportunity or good news which you have been eagerly awaiting. It will come but in its own sweet time. During this trying time, avoid stepping on people's toes. Getting desperate or forcing people to take a decision favourable to you will only push your luck away.

August

You will be your own greatest adversary this August. The situation could get difficult for you and your co-workers in general will let you down. They will disregard your work and try to take the credit due to you. But negative thoughts and resentment towards these people will only make the situation worse. Don't let these personal remarks pull you down so much that you begin to create problems for yourself. Instead be patient and tolerant and let this phase pass. It will settle down in time.

Unfortunately, I see you feeling restless and spending sleepless nights worried about your work and your job security. But all these negative thoughts are only in your head. If you think objectively you will realize that this issue is not as serious as you are making it out to be. You are making a mountain out of a molehill. Calm down and see the situation improve. The month will end with some positive developments, and these instances will only increase if you begin to approach your work less seriously and learn to have some fun. All work and no play will make you a dull person.

September

Your work will look exceptionally good at the start of this month. You may undertake international travel and explore opportunities which could give you an international placement. Your work will be on an upswing and I see you happy and completely in harmony with your work. I see you ready to take up a new initiative which is unlike anything you have done before. You have a thrilling adventure ahead of you and there is a lot you can learn and enjoy from this experience. You will be highly driven and goal-oriented for this initiative.

Towards the end of the month, you will be serious about your work goals and will be ready to execute the tasks assigned to you. At some point you will realize that you are capable of success and that you will achieve victory over all odds.

October

You may face some sort of defeat this month. The people around you may disregard and disrespect your work and take credit for what you have done. This will leave you disheartened and stressed. Mid-month, you will be eagerly waiting for decisions or opportunities that depend on other people. Unfortunately, there will be some delay in these, and your patience will be tested. Stay calm and let time take its course.

The month will end with some amount of boredom arising in your work. You will lose interest and may begin to see only the negative aspects of your career. Instead, if you focus on the bright side of your career, you may attract what you desire.

November

You will have to take some difficult decisions which will involve ending your association with an ongoing job, client or project. You have done everything in your capacity to change the situation, but your efforts have been futile. Your best option is to end this association and move on in pursuit of your passion. You could consider relocating for a better job or career prospect. This will be a good decision in the present scheme of things.

Later in the month, you could be stuck in a situation of imbalance where you are torn between two aspects of work. This may mean two jobs, two people or two assignments which will begin to take their toll on you. You have the energy to handle only one of them. So make a quick choice and move on. Keeping two swords in the same sheath is not recommended. The month will end in a phase with your work situation getting difficult. You may be overwhelmed, tired and may feel defeated and would be considering giving up all that you have earned so far to escape this gruelling phase. But fleeing would be cowardice and I suggest you hang in there, fight on – and you will see victory.

December

This December, you will receive the results for all the hard work you put in last month. You will witness positive outcomes and the situation at work will improve. Your effort will be noticed and your contribution acknowledged. Appreciation and rewards will begin to flow in now. If you are looking for work, a good offer will come through this month. I see you juggling your work with your personal life. This multitasking may seem stressful but it is your only way to achieve work/life balance in the present situation. Respite will come soon.

Towards the end of the month, when you look back at the year gone by, I see that you may have feelings of regret and remorse. There is something about the past that is bothering you, and you could be taking many of your present decisions based on what occurred in the past. In my opinion, you should drop this emotional baggage which has become an impediment to your progress. It is important that you start the new year with a clean slate.

The Spiritual You

Spirituality is a topic that is very close to my heart. This section has been created to give you a perspective of how your year will look if you choose to focus on your spiritual side. This spiritual side, in my opinion, will enable you to awaken your soul. How many of us go beyond this body? How many of us even go beyond the mind? Well, spirituality is a realm which goes beyond the body and the mind. It goes to that point of your existence that connects you directly with the universe. And this point that connects your body or your mind or you with this larger universe is called the soul. The soul is called 'atma' in Hindi, ever powerful, immortal, the greatest creation of the divine entity. It is the single most important aspect which connects you to this large universe.

How else would it be possible for people who are reborn after death to remember events of their past life or past births? It is simply because your soul travels through time, through space, through you in the various forms that you take from one birth to another; through all this, your atma remains the same. The ultimate purpose of this soul is to come into the oneness of the universe; this oneness can be achieved through self-realization, also called 'nirvana'. When the Buddha attained enlightenment, he didn't become a god or a magician, he simply became a man who, through the scientific concept of meditation, achieved mindfulness. Mindfulness means awareness of the present moment. When one attains total awareness he/she becomes free from moha (desire), the root cause of suffering, pain and sadness.

You picked up this book with the intention to find out if your year ahead could be happier than the previous one. Well, this is where the buck stops. Look into your spiritual realm and you will begin to discover that happiness lies within and not without. For now, I give you your spiritual predictions for 2018 and thereafter, in the final section of this book, you will see a very interesting note on how this awareness can change your life. I call this section the USP of my book. This is a very special section which has an edge over the other sections because it speaks to your soul.

We are often trapped in the superficial aspects of our lives – wealth, career, power, security, etc. Spirituality, the most important aspect, is out of place here. This is my attempt to connect you with your soul and to show you your spiritual side and your true potential. Spirituality is natural to every being, but we never look at it. This reading of the four quarters of 2018 will take you through your spiritual achievements and help you explore the path less taken.

January–March

The year will start off remarkably well and you will experience glimpses of your spiritual awakening. You will begin to experience a strong sense of calm and peace within yourself as time progresses. This calm feeling is a sign of mindfulness and is a great achievement. You will begin to adopt this calm and peaceful approach in your daily routine and may see some fabulous outcomes emerge from it. This is a great start to your spiritual quest and I hope you keep it going.

As the first quarter progresses, you may encounter a man who is experienced and knowledgeable. He will guide you on your spiritual path and answer all your questions which have remained unanswered for a long time now. Your thoughts will be aligned towards achieving more awareness in your daily life and developing your spiritual practice. You will be focused on achieving your spiritual goals and will continue to make the progress which I witnessed in your reading in January.

As time goes by, you will become more and more aware of your spiritual awakening and you will realize that you are no longer the mindless thinker but an alert observer. This transition will give you a lot of power over yourself and your ego. You will begin to hone this skill of awareness and use it in your daily life. This may be a good time to mentor others or at least help others see their spiritual side. You could also help others understand what their purpose is and simply guide them to become aware of their inner being.

April–June

April will be a month for patience and resilience. You may be getting impatient after your early achievements in the first quarter and looking for more glimpses of spiritual awakening this month. But the more eager you are for this spiritual awakening, the more unsuccessful you will be. Your best option would be to focus on being aware of the present moment. Become intensely aware of where you are instead of wasting the present moment on thinking of the past or the future. Don't resist what is, but accept what you have right now. When you surrender to the moment that you are in, you will witness the spiritual awakening you did in the last quarter. Don't go seeking it; it will come to you when you are ready.

I see you losing interest in your spiritual practice in May. You will want quick results at this time, but spirituality is all about patience and steady and continuous work. You can't work on it one day and leave it the next day. You need to work consistently to develop awareness. The more you chase it, the further it will move away. Thus, don't lose your focus and definitely don't lose sight of your spiritual goals.

In June, you may realize that the spiritual or religious beliefs that you thought were true may actually be false. This revelation may be an eye-opener for you. Also, be wary of people who claim to be spiritual leaders but may cheat you. Don't be gullible and fall for everything that comes in the name of spirituality. Research it well and dispel any doubts.

July–September

You may be worried about what other people think of your spiritual progress. The desire to win the approval of others may compel you to change your spiritual focus. In my opinion what eventually matters is what you think and believe in, not how other people perceive you. You need to establish your own spiritual path. The experiences you have on this journey and what you learn will be relevant to you and no one else. Spirituality is not acquired but experienced. Hence, keep your experiences to yourself and don't seek approval from others.

As the quarter progresses, your hope may dwindle and your faith in your spiritual quest may weaken. But tarot indicates that you will have to stay strong and believe in your spiritual progress at this time. I don't see results coming your way now. You will see results only if you believe completely in your ultimate goal. The quarter will end with you taking up a new initiative on your spiritual path. You may take up a class or a course or join a group of like-minded people who come together to share their experiences. This will help you learn about spirituality and grow as a person. By the end of September, you will be ready to forsake your old beliefs gleaned from other people and adopt new ones which will be your own. You will walk the spiritual path in the manner that you desire. This in itself will be a spiritual awakening and a victory for you.

October–December

You are advised to stay away from unscrupulous people; do not trust them with your spiritual beliefs or take advice from them for your spiritual journey. This October, you may face treachery or deception from one such person who may have cheated you in the name of spirituality. But all you can do is to put this bad experience behind you and continue to move forward towards your goal of spiritual awakening. You must learn to be more vigilant and informed in the future.

This deceit will leave you hurt and disappointed and may prompt you to take a break from your spiritual quest. This break in November will be short but it will serve you well as it will help you acquire a fresh perspective about spirituality and your life in general. After all the stress you have experienced, some respite is necessary. You could simply take a break to do nothing and just be with yourself in the present moment. Just doing this will give you much-needed clarity.

In December, you may begin to get impatient for rewards in the form of spiritual awakening. But like I said before, the more you chase this goal, the more it will move away from you. Hence, it is important that you focus on the path and not the destination. You will receive your reward and it will be exceptionally sweet but don't get impatient for it. Just stay in the moment and continue to be mindful.

Author's Note

This is my favourite section in the book because I get to write about things which are beyond predictions here. In fact, what I write in this section deals with the basis of existence. I will only discuss the importance of living in the moment, mindfulness and the adverse effects of mindlessness here. I have discussed anicca (impermanence) and apranahita (aimlessness) in previous books and will discuss another interesting concept or a theory associated with mindfulness in this book – the concept of 'no mind'.

I first learnt about no mind from the book *Zen Mind, Beginner's Mind*. What I love about this book is the way it presents the concept of no mind. No mind means a mind without the mind! Complicated isn't it? During the read, if you don't understand something or have questions, please feel free to drop me an email at karmel@tarotreader.in and I will be delighted to answer them or clarify your doubts.

Part I: What is No Mind?
Part II: Benefits of No Mind
Part III: Ways to Achieve No Mind

Part I

What is No Mind?

I first heard about this concept in the film *The Last Samurai*. In the film, this concept is referred to as the basis of creation, the basis of life of the samurais. The film discusses how being in no mind can actually help you achieve what you desire, and even help you attain salvation. Later I read up on this concept and discovered that no mind means the space in your mind where your mind doesn't exist or is empty. This is the part of the mind which does not have ego, or the emotions of anger, desire, fear, love or hate. Can you imagine a time, even for a second, when you are free from the constant chattering in your mind? I am sure you have never experienced this state. But if you do think about this concept and do the work required, you may be able to glimpse the no mind zone.

Whenever I can't sleep, I find I can hear my thoughts of fear and insecurity, pain and misery so loudly that they actually bother me. At times like this, I usually give up trying to sleep and simply give in to my chattering mind. This makes me the slave of my mind. You may be doing this too, when you are restless and unable to sleep. The mind is a formidable opponent. It is hard to defeat and will not go down without a fight.

The only way to train your mind to listen to you, to submit to you, is to create empty spaces in it; in other words, create a no mind zone. No mind is the state when thoughts don't exist, when you are open to everything, unlike in the normal state when your mind tends to latch on to thoughts and manipulates them. Let's try to understand how your mind behaves normally by looking at the example below:

Imagine you get a call from your boss and he tells you: 'Hey listen, I want to talk to you about something important. This may not be such great news and I hope you take it well. Let me know when you are here and we can chat up.'

While you are listening to this conversation, you may start having horrific thoughts, such as: 'Chat up means what? Am I going to be fired? Oh God, yes I am going to be fired! No job means no money; I will default on my mortgage payment;

I can't buy the car now; how will I pay my bills? My kid's school fees are not going to be paid! Oh God, I am doomed, I am a loser; What do I tell my wife/husband? What do I tell my friends? I will never find a job in time, it will take me a year to find a job that pays me this much! I am dead meat, I am doomed.'

These thoughts of anger, dejection and disappointment are all symptoms of a state which is just the opposite of no mind. Observe how your mind drove you to assume what your boss was planning to say to you. You simply jumped to conclusions. You have no idea what your boss is going to discuss with you, but your mind has led you to focus on the worst case scenario such as being fired! If you have had thoughts of this kind in other situations, then you know how you are enslaved to your mind and its incessant chattering.

Now if you were in the no mind zone, you are likely to have handled the comment from your boss in the following way:

While you are listening to your boss talking, you will be fully present in the moment. You will be devoid of any prejudice, anger, resentment or thought. You will simply be listening. At the end of the call you will simply smile with amusement, wondering what your boss wants to discuss. You won't dissect the information he provided, neither will you judge it as good or bad. What the discussion will be about, what will be its outcome, doesn't concern you at all. You will put the phone down and resume what you were doing – maybe washing the dishes – before the call.

You will resume doing the dishes mindfully, and feel the water on your fingers and the foam of the liquid soap, and focus on rinsing the dishes. You will not reflect on the call you just received. You will simply be in the no mind zone in which you are not attached to any thoughts, not disturbed by negative ideas nor are you feeling joyous because of positive thoughts. This is how you are in a state of no mind – when the mind is quiet and calm, focused on the task assigned to it.

Part II

Benefits of No Mind

You will benefit greatly when you achieve no mind, even if it is for a second. Imagine a minute of no thought, no tension, no worries, no pain and no fear. Simply an empty mind! In such a state you can achieve eternal happiness. Unfortunately, the only people who seem to practise no mind are the monks. If you speak to them, you will realize how detached they are from worldly desires, which makes them calm and peaceful.

You can begin to practise no mind by taking small steps. Through this practice, you will achieve moments of bliss and learn to calmly handle the stressors in your life. No mind teaches you to approach concepts in a detached manner, without any inhibitions and illusions. You simply look at everything from the perspective of a third person and are not affected by situations, problems or difficulties. You become the watcher, the observer who sees an emotion without identifying with it.

When you begin to observe your thoughts, you begin to exert control over your mind. You begin to drive your thoughts from a negative standpoint to a positive one. You begin to control your emotions. Whether you are feeling happy or sad, you will be aware of what is happening inside you. This gives you power over your mind. The next time you are in a difficult situation, start observing the mindless chattering in your mind and simply smile at it. As you begin to observe this noise in your head in a detached manner, your negative or positive emotions will disappear.

You could be involved in a situation where someone is screaming or pointing fingers at you. If you are in a state of no mind, you will begin to look at this person as someone who is cursing your ego and trying to attach your mind. You will look at this person as someone who is wounded and needs to vent to feel better. You will begin to feel good that you could help this person because he/she could vent to you. You will begin to detach from your ego and, therefore, your mind.

Your mind will have control over you as long as your ego is involved. The moment the ego or I, me and mine disappears from your identity, your mind will no longer have power over you. You will then simply be in the present moment, where fears and inhibitions don't matter, where good and bad don't have any importance, neither does wealth. You become enlightened, and this realization that you have power over your mind becomes your greatest tool to achieve success.

If you start watching your thoughts and not identifying with them, you will achieve the following benefits:

- Anger and ego will lose their power over you. You will no longer have a bloated ego, nor will your tongue work faster than your thoughts. You will have control over both.
- Love, hatred, pain, misery and other emotions of this kind will have no impact on you.
- You will be calm in your approach and handle situations logically and practically.
- You will have greater clarity and your purpose will begin to surface.
- You will see beyond I, me and myself.
- You will be separated from yourself. You will become the watcher and will no longer be the thinker.
- You will have power over your feelings, emotions and thoughts.

The experience of no mind will vary from person to person. You can judge its potential only after you begin to attain this state. To do that you need to learn how to achieve no mind.

Part III

How to Achieve No Mind

You cannot achieve a no mind state overnight. It takes years and years of steady practice. Therefore, instead of attaining nirvana your focus should be on attaining a calm and composed demeanour so that you have positive thoughts and are able to channelize your energy into achieving a happy outcome. Everyone wants to be happy – new cars, a big home, a fat pay check, a hefty bank balance, are all aimed at enhancing happiness. But happiness is actually a state of mind. It is the result of no mind.

The following steps will help you align your mind to no mind:

1. Observe every thought; take note of your emotions

This is easier said than done. Your first reaction to any situation will be to identify with the situation and immediately get carried away by the chatter of the mind. Well this is the challenge – the moment such nonsensical blabbering begins in your head, stop and watch it like an external observer. If you do this often, you will begin to realize that when you observe a thought or a feeling, it loses its power over you. The more you tune in to your thoughts and feelings, the more easily you begin to detach yourself from them.

2. Walking, washing or driving meditation

Who says that meditation can only be done while you are sitting still in one place? Most people believe that meditation is boring and slow. Instead of practising sitting meditation which is tough to do initially, you can practise something that comes more naturally to you, e.g. walking meditation.

You can do this when you are out for your daily walk. Simply watch every step you take. Observe how one leg goes up and the other stays down. Feel the pressure when your feet touch the ground. Count each step you take and name them – left down, right down, etc. This way you will be mindful while walking which will prevent your mind from wandering. If your mind does wander to the past or the future, gently bring it back to the present and begin counting each step again.

You can even try this approach while you are driving or washing dishes. Every time you are at the wheel, name every activity you perform while driving, such as accelerate, brake, etc. When your mind wanders, name it and gently bring it back to where it should be. Similarly, name what you do while washing dishes. This way your mind will gradually come under your control and you will know when it wanders.

3. Experiencing No Mind

After continuous practice of being the observer, you will begin to experience empty spaces. This may happen any time, for instance while you are having a cup of coffee. You may have no other thought in your mind at this time, except for the enjoyment of the coffee. You will be able to smell its aroma taste its rich flavour and hear the gulping sound with every sip. This is when you will begin to notice the calm state of your mind, which is no mind.

This state of mindfulness may not last longer than the time you take to drink the cup of coffee, but it will show you what true happiness feels like. You may also experience this state of no mind when you are listening to a pleasant song. As you begin to enjoy this state of no mind – when the mind is asleep but you are awake and alert – you will try to achieve it more often.

4. Books that can help you attain No Mind

I especially recommend the first two titles:

Zen Mind, Beginners Mind, by Shunryu Suzuki

An Introduction to Zen Buddhism, by D.T. Suzuki

Zen Doctrine of No Mind, by D.T. Suzuki

Zen: The Quantum Leap From Mind to No Mind, by Osho

Essays in Zen Buddhism, by D.T. Suzuki

Zen Buddhism and Psychoanalysis, by Erich Fromm, D.T Suzuki, Richard De Martino

Mindfulness in Plain English, by Bhante Henepola Gunaratana

You are Here, by Thich Nhat Hanh

The Miracle of Mindfulness, by Thich Nhat Hanh

A Guide to Awareness, by Somdet Phra Nyanasamvara

Being Peace, by Thich Nhat Hanh

Be Free Where You Are, by Thich Nhat Hanh

Intuitive Awareness, by Ajahn Sumedho

The Diamond Sutra, by Osho

Dhamma Discourses on Vipassana Meditation, by Ven. Sayadaw Kundala

Becoming Your Own Therapist & Make Your Mind an Ocean, by Lama Thubten Yeshe

The Art of Living, by Ven. Master Chin Kung

Practical Insight Meditation, by Ven. Mahasi Sayadaw

Taming the Monkey Mind, by Cheng Wei-an

Cutting Through Spiritual Materialism, by Chogyam Trungpa

Lankavatara Sutra (Source – Buddhanet.net)

With this I end my journey with you this year.

Acknowledgements

This book is a product of my hard work, knowledge and dedication to tarot. I would like to thank the universe for giving me this opportunity to bring the magical power of tarot to you in the form of this book. My mission is to make tarot a household name and the universe has helped me in every aspect to achieve this. I would like to thank my beloved husband Manoj Nair for his support, and my daughter Miara for her patience and love. They are my pillars who have supported me to become what I am today. Finally, I would like to thank my publisher HarperCollins for giving me this brilliant opportunity to reveal the magic of tarot through this book. One other important person who has helped me with my book is Bidisha Srivastava and I would like to thank her for the efforts she has put in as an editor and my guide. She has worked with me since the time the books were conceived. My books are as much her success as mine. I hope you enjoy unravelling your future through it.